15

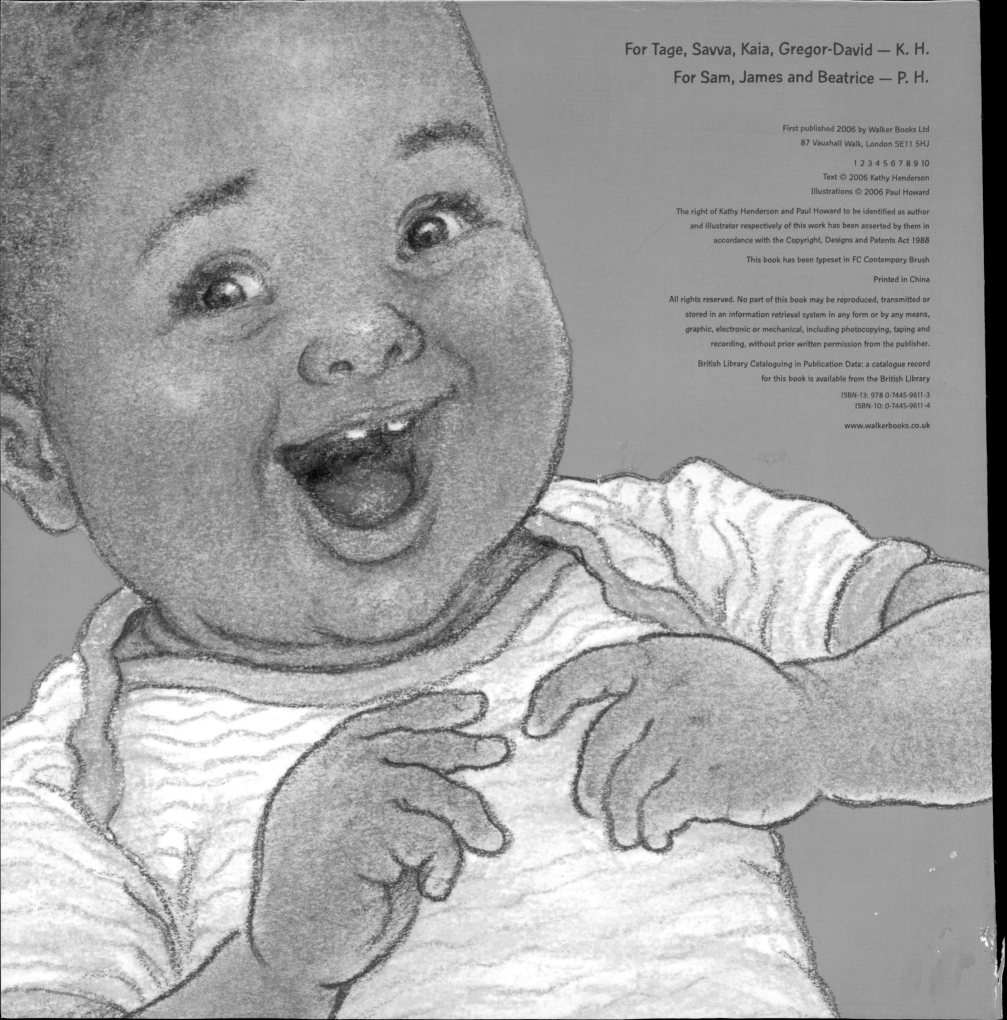

For Tage, Savva, Kaia, Gregor-David — K. H.

For Sam, James and Beatrice — P. H.

First published 2006 by Walker Books Ltd

87 Vauxhall Walk, London SE11 5HJ

1 2 3 4 5 6 7 8 9 10

Text © 2006 Kathy Henderson

Illustrations © 2006 Paul Howard

This book has been typeset in FC Contempory Brush

Printed in China

British Library Cataloguing in Publication Data: a catalogue record for this book is available from the British Library

ISBN-13: 978 0-7445-9611-3

ISBN-10: 0-7445-9611-4

www.walkerbooks.co.uk

LOOK AT YOU!

A Baby Body Book

KATHY HENDERSON illustrated by PAUL HOWARD

WALKER BOOKS
AND SUBSIDIARIES
LONDON · BOSTON · SYDNEY · AUCKLAND

Fingers and toes wiggle.

Eyes, nose and mouth giggle.

Arms wave, legs kick ...

bottoms squirm ...
and tummies tickle.

Clothes on.

Where's the baby gone?

There
he is!

Clothes off!

Where are the baby's toes?

There they are!

Lie

roll

sit

wobble.

Rock

crawl

pull

wobble.

Stand

wobble

sway

wobble.

Bump!

Step

walk

toddle!

What can you see?

Something to eat.

What can you hear?

A song in the air.

And how does it feel?

Warm and squelchy, scratchy, rough, sticky, squishy...

Time for a bath!

Float   soap

splash

wash

cuddle

brush.

Clip, snip, some things grow quick.

Hey ho, others grow slow!

Funny thing, hair...
You can brush it this way,
you can brush it that,
wash it, dry it, tie it up
and squash it flat.

I feel ...
good,

bad,

happy,

sad,

bold,

shy
(I don't
know why).

I want yours!

No! It's mine!

I feel
lonely.

I feel
fine.

A-a-a-chooo!

Wow, what a body can do!

Yawn! Hic!

Plenty of tricks.

Whoops!
Pooh!

Wow, what a body can do!

Sigh, flop, snuggle down,
curl up in a heap.

The story's done, this body's tired
and now it's going to sleep.